45 WAYS DONALD TRUMP COLLUDED WITH RUSSIA

And Destroyed American Politics

Maxwell Lane

This book is dedicated to the truth.

Author's Note

All information included in this book is factual*, and based on a report by Robert Mueller. Countless hours were dedicated to discovering the answer to one of America's greatest secrets. I encourage you to do your own independent research in order to validate all information presented.

*There is no need to debate semantics. This is only a satire.

CHAPTER 1

H^{e didn't.}

Maxwell Lane

CHAPTER 2

He didn't.

CHAPTER 3

H e didn't.

CHAPTER 4

He didn't.

CHAPTER 5

H^{e didn't.}

CHAPTER 6

He didn't.

◆ ◆ ◆

CHAPTER 7

H e didn't.

CHAPTER 8

H^{e didn't.}

He didn't.

CHAPTER 9

H e didn't.

CHAPTER 10

H^{e didn't.}

CHAPTER 11

H^{e didn't.}

CHAPTER 12

He didn't.

CHAPTER 13

He didn't.

CHAPTER 14

H e didn't.

CHAPTER 15

H^{e didn't.}

CHAPTER 16

H^{e didn't.}

He didn't.

◆ ◆ ◆

CHAPTER 17

H^{e didn't.}

CHAPTER 18

H^{e didn't.}

CHAPTER 19

He didn't.

CHAPTER 20

He didn't.

CHAPTER 21

He didn't.

CHAPTER 22

He didn't.

CHAPTER 23

He didn't.

CHAPTER 24

He didn't.

CHAPTER 25

H^{e didn't.}

CHAPTER 26

H e didn't.

CHAPTER 27

H^{e didn't.}

CHAPTER 28

H^{e didn't.}

❖ ❖ ❖

CHAPTER 29

He didn't.

CHAPTER 30

He didn't.

CHAPTER 31

H^{e didn't.}

CHAPTER 32

H^{e didn't.}

He didn't.

◆ ◆ ◆

CHAPTER 33

H^{e didn't.}

◆ ◆ ◆

CHAPTER 34

He didn't.

◆ ◆ ◆

CHAPTER 35

He didn't.

CHAPTER 36

H^{e didn't.}

◆ ◆ ◆

CHAPTER 37

H e didn't.

CHAPTER 38

H^{e didn't.}

CHAPTER 39

H^{e didn't.}

CHAPTER 40

H^{e didn't.}

CHAPTER 41

He didn't.

CHAPTER 42

H e didn't.

CHAPTER 43

H^{e didn't.}

CHAPTER 44

He didn't.

CHAPTER 45

Donald Trump is the 45th President of the United States of America.